THE 'PRAYING WITH SCRIPTURE' PROGRAMME

Leader's Guide

MICHAEL AND TERRI QUINN

FAMILY CARING TRUST

First published 1991
by Family Caring Trust
44 Rathfriland Road
Newry
Co. Down
BT34 1LD
Tel Newry 64174

Copyright © Family Caring Trust, 1991
ISBN 1872253 05 9

Illustrations and design: Pauline McGrath
Typesetting: Cassidy Printers, Newry
Printing: Universities Press (Belfast)

Bible text is reproduced from the
Good News Bible © American Bible Society,
New York, 1966, 1971 and 4th edition 1976,
published by the Bible Societies/
Harper Harper Collins, with permission.

CONTENTS

INTRODUCTION

The Materials

This is the Leader's Guide for a flexible course introducing various methods of praying with Scripture. The Guide contains all the information needed for setting up the programme and conducting each session of it. It is designed to be used in conjunction with the handbook for participants 'Enjoy Praying.'

The handbook contains the input and Scripture passage for each session, also the passages from Scripture for participants to pray on between sessions. A number of existing courses on prayer do not include a participant's handbook, which seems a pity, for a handbook can facilitate and reinforce learning both between sessions and long after a course has finished. A handbook also helps to answer the need for some solid catechesis on prayer and spirituality in addition to giving people an experience of prayer.

A copy of the handbook is supplied to each participant. It is not expensive, but embarrassment can be avoided when a 'secret bag' is passed around at the end of each session. People can put what they wish into the bag to cover the cost of handbooks, notebooks, etc.

The purpose of the course

It is in praying that we learn to pray. We learn, not by reading about prayer or hearing about it, but by **trying** it. The purpose of the course is to allow people to experience a variety of methods of prayer so that they may discover what works best for themselves and what suits their individual personalities.

The emphasis in the course is on improving communication with God. But prayer is not just a matter of communication skills that can be learnt from others. God alone can teach us to pray (St Paul tells us that it is the Spirit that prays within us). Yet faulty communication — lack of listening, mistaken images of God and of ourselves, lack of honesty about our feelings, lack of appreciation and thanks — are basic flaws that can prevent us from being open to the Spirit working in us and enabling us to pray effectively. Hence the emphasis on communication.

Prayer and family life

As well as introducing people to various methods of praying with scripture, the course has a family spirituality focus. It aims to help people to find ways of letting their prayer overflow onto the practical details of daily living and loving in their families and in other relationships. After all, prayer is not just a personal luxury. It needs to overflow onto the people who are closest to us — particularly our own families whom God has called us to love in a special way.

Some people may object that there is a greater need for a course on **family** prayer rather than on individual prayer. That is a great need. But family prayer could be a bit superficial — rather like window dressing — if parents were not first praying and growing in friendship with God themselves. In that sense, this course might be seen as a foundation for family prayer.

Objections to a family emphasis

Teenagers or young adults may wonder about this emphasis on family. They may object that an important task in their lives at present is actually to **separate** from family and begin to prepare for forming a family of their own. If they only come home at weekends, or if they live at home but find that their friends are now much more important to them than their families, they may resent an emphasis on family relationships. And they may very well be right. Certainly, Jesus warned us against a too narrow care for family that puts family first in every circumstance. So encourage people to adapt these ideas to their own situation. But it may help to bear in mind that the way young people treat their parents, sisters and brothers tends to be the way they will treat their husband/ wife/ children in the future. For they are now establishing patterns of encouraging or criticising, of taking on responsibilities or shirking them, of co-operating with family members and being a friend to them, or ignoring them — and these patterns quickly become lifelong habits. While it is important to pray about their new friends and responsibilities, it may also be important to pray about their family relationships too. Prayer can thus help them to develop more open communication at home, to express their needs, and to talk out chores and responsibilities.

Older people living alone will need to be equally flexible in adapting these ideas. Again, it may help them to bear in mind that God's plan for them is to form loving relationships with those who are closest to them, so they may like to apply the word 'family' to the little community of their neighbours and friends.

How the programme works

The idea of the programme, then, is to enable small groups of people to come together and support each other as they practise a variety of methods of praying. No number is too small — this can be a do-it-yourself course for one individual or couple — but there is great mutual enrichment in a larger group of up to ten people. It is not recommended that you go over ten. Where possible, groups meet in comfortable, pleasant surroundings, often in someone's home, if it is reasonably free from distractions.

In the programme there are six sessions, held at weekly intervals. The six sessions correspond to the first six chapters of the participant's handbook. Each session lasts about one and a half hours, and it generally goes like this (times approximate):

1. A brief introduction. (5 mins)

2. How everyone got on since the previous meeting. (20-30 mins)

3. The new topic is introduced — based on the 'Tips' at the end of the chapter. (5-10 mins)

4. Quietening down/ centring. (6-7 mins)

5. Praying with a story from the Gospels. (20-30 mins)

6. Feedback and summing up. (5-10 mins)

7. Homework and concluding remarks. (3-4 mins).

These different sections are explained in the outlines for each session in this book.

Leading a course

The programme is designed to run itself. Because of the detail in the handbook and the Leader's Guide, and because of the structure of the course, it does not require an expert facilitator. As a presenter, therefore, it is important for you to understand that you are not there as a teacher but as a fellow-learner and a fellow pray-er — even praying on the same passages as the other participants during each week. This can be particularly important in groups of young people, where the participants may find it more difficult to relate to an adult (though, in that case, it may also be helpful for an older person to share the leadership with a young adult).

The story of the two beggars, told on the first evening of the course, (see Session One), embodies the right attitude. As leaders, we must not see ourselves as 'experts' on prayer, but as needy people. It is an important image, for it helps to explain how people leading courses can be effective without being experts. They are merely sharing from what has been given to them by others.

Two presenters normally share the leadership of a group. It is not just because this enables them to share the burden and responsibility of running a group, but also because it is a great help to have two experienced people in a group whose sharing raises the standard and models different methods of prayer. That sharing can be a great inspiration to people doing a course.

You are encouraged, then, to share with the group how you are getting on with prayer — the downs as well as the ups. Better still if you share the **effects** of your prayer — on your daily life at home, at work, and in the community, but especially the effect on your marriage and the way you treat your family.

It is essential that you be committed to prayer and to practising some of the methods introduced on the course. Those who have run the course have also emphasised the value of time spent preparing before each session.

What the leader does

One of the most important qualities in a facilitator is respect — even reverence — for people and for the different ways in which they meet God. It is particularly important to respect people's own pace and instincts, and

8

to avoid adding any new burdens of guilt, for there is not just one way to pray. Respect their fears of sharing, too, or of speaking publicly — always give them the right to pass. Some of them may feel uncomfortable with silence, especially during the first session — which is one reason for playing instrumental music (but not familiar tunes) in the background during times of quietening down and prayer. And don't worry if some people have a good deal of difficulty in praying on the various passages for the first weeks — or even for the duration of the course. They are **learning** to pray, and that does not normally happen overnight. They can always go through the exercises again at their own pace when the course has finished.

Experiment to find what helps you to get people to talk more honestly and freely. If someone says they found it difficult to pray during the previous week, it may help to say something like: 'So prayer wasn't easy this week...' Reflecting back in your own words what they have just said usually encourages them to say more. But avoid asking direct questions — 'Did you not make the time to pray, then?' as that is threatening rather than helpful.

Dealing with objections

Inevitably, some people will ask you questions or look to you for answers. How can you deal with that? One good way is to ask questioners if they have talked to God about the problem themselves — 'Do you tell the Lord how you feel about this? — and to help them to see that it's important to bring our questions and difficulties to God. Apart from that, it often helps to turn the question back: 'What do you think yourself?' or 'What do you think Jesus would say?' — anything that respects people and encourages them to open themselves up to the Holy Spirit working in very different ways in each one.

Another useful way of dealing with questions — and objections! — is to open the question out to the group. You might ask: "I wonder what's the experience of the rest of the group? What has anyone else found?" The sharing of that experience can be very powerful.

Feel free to share your own experience too, especially when someone begins to intellectualise or to raise objections? For example, if someone

9

says 'It seems to me that the Father treated the elder son very unfairly!' you might talk about your own struggles or experiences in that area, even acknowledging, perhaps, that you also used to think it was unfair. That approach is particularly useful in enabling people to get away from theory and abstract ideas, and to talk at the much more helpful personal level.

How are leaders trained?

The training of leaders for this programme follows the principles of the programme itself — that it is in praying that we learn to pray. A good way to start is to get together with a number of potential leaders — perhaps people who have already been leading parenting courses or who belong to an existing group — and try the course out for yourself. (People doing any kind of community work need enrichment and stimulation in any case, and they should at least be given the opportunity to serve their community in a **different** way after a number of years). Such a course can take place in the privacy of your home, and the leadership can be revolved among those who are willing. That has already proven effective as a way to start, for it gives people the experience of prayer, a conviction about its importance, and familiarity with the content and structure of the programme.

Obviously, ongoing support will also be very useful if people are to continue to grow in prayer. Thankfully, this is being provided increasingly by Churches at diocesan level, and by church-related organisations like Scripture Union, Charismatic Renewal, Siol, etc. An occasional day of renewal that includes both input and some experience of prayer can be a great help.

Recruiting

There is considerable demand from existing prayer groups for a structured course on prayer. Also from parish groups, youth groups, church organisations, lay ministry groups, scripture study groups, parish councils, etc. Many of these are constantly on the look-out for a structure and content for their gatherings that can offer them further enrichment. Similarly, the course may be used as a Lenten programme or as a practical training for those who read Scripture in church.

It would be a pity, however, to see praying with Scripture as something for the elite or the 'converted.' The Good News is for everyone. But how do you reach people who feel little need for this kind of enrichment? It would appear that one of the best ways is to offer the course to people who have already taken part in other community programmes and have enjoyed them. There is a strong demand from parents, for example, for follow-up to a parenting programme, and that can provide ready-made groups. This demand comes even from people who may not have been particularly interested in prayer or things spiritual. Once they have had the liberating experience of learning in a trusting group of people, they often find that they have new horizons and are more open to new experiences. And if the course they have done was provided by their local church or a church school, their experience of the church caring about their children seems to leave them even more open to prayer support.

Some parents specifically express the need for help with prayer, including family prayer. There are many books on prayer already available, of course. But people seem to learn much better when they come together in a safe, structured setting. In this way they gain strength and support from each other, and they find they can learn better.

Preparing the participants

We would emphasise that people must be encouraged to come voluntarily. This needs to be borne in mind particularly in the school context. If the programme is being used for young adults, it needs to be freely entered into and should not be presented as part of a class, or during school hours. Some students who did the course after school even reported that they would have felt more comfortable if they had not been wearing school uniforms.

At the back of this book, there is a sample letter inviting people to experience the programme. You may use or adapt it as you wish. It also spells out the commitment to pray every day while the course lasts. That is important to the success of the course, so people need to be made aware of that commitment **in advance**.

If you really believe in the power of prayer, then you will probably want to organise people to pray for the participants on each course you run. Many facilitators arrange for people in their community to pray specifically for the group, sometimes one person for each individual.

Flexibility

You are encouraged to try this programme the way it is the first time you run it. Some exercises may seem unusual or strange when you read them, yet they often prove very successful when they are actually tried in a group. That said, you know your own community and will have a natural sensitivity to the needs of people within it. In some Protestant groups, for example, lighting a candle may be so far from the tradition of some of the participants that it will not be appropriate; in other groups, the secret bag may remind people too much of a church collection! So be flexible and don't insist on details that might upset people or prevent them from experiencing what is important on the course. Feel free to adapt and change the outline, especially as you gain experience. It **needs** to be adapted to different kinds of groups and situations.

You may prefer, for example, to use a different form of centring down by taking some of the exercises from the early part of Anthony de Mello's book 'Sadhana.' And don't feel that you have to follow the script rigidly, especially if it takes from your own spontaneity. Some people prefer to read it for ideas and then make their own of it. Times, too, are only approximate.

Another area where you may need to be flexible is in the use of group work. When the outline suggests a question for sharing by the full group, for example, there will be times when it it may be better to work in threes rather than make people feel uncomfortable speaking in front of the larger group.

As you adapt the programme, you may find better ways of explaining something or of helping people to have a positive experience of prayer. At Family Caring Trust, we are always pleased to hear from you about your experience of leading courses, and your feedback can be incorporated into future editions of the programme. So good luck with the course, and please do not hesitate to send us your feedback.

SESSION ONE

Checklist

Handbooks (one per person);

Bible, opened in a central position, perhaps on a coffee-table in the middle;

Cassette with suitable instrumental music, and cassette player;

This leader's guide;

Two handmade posters ('Introducing self' and Outline, see below) & adhesive;

Reading light (it can help the atmosphere during sharing and during prayer exercises to switch off the main light and use only a reading light).

Candle and matches;

'Secret bag' for donations, if appropriate — perhaps a glove!

inexpensive copy-books (one per person)

Arrange chairs loosely in a circle

1. Introduction (30-40 minutes)

The goal of this session is to introduce people to each other, to help them begin to feel comfortable with each other, to relax them and calm any fears they may have, also to introduce them to the format of each session and give them an actual experience of prayer.

I'd like to make you very welcome — I appreciate your trust in coming along and I hope that, like most people, you'll find this an enjoyable, relaxing and helpful experience.

I'll begin by explaining what it's all about, so you'll know what to expect. The purpose of the course is to introduce you to simple methods of praying with the New Testament and give you an actual experience of that. There are many forms of prayer, and you are encouraged to continue to use whatever form of prayer you may have found helpful in the past, but prayer with the Bible is a very rich way of praying which this course introduces.

The course (or 'retreat,' as some prefer to call it) has six sessions, once a week — I wonder if this time and day of the week is suitable for you all?....

Now I'm not an expert on prayer. There's a story told of two men who met along the road. Both were beggars. Both were poor. But one of them knew where food could be got, and he told his friend. It's in that spirit that this course is offered. None of these methods of prayer is original or new. They are all tried and tested methods that we have learned, and are still learning, from others. We are just here to lead you through the different sections of each session; we're following an outline, and looking forward to learning along with you.

Put up a home-made poster for the "introducing ourselves" exercise which follows:

My name...
My family (brothers, sisters, parents, children...)
Why I'm doing this course.
What I wouldn't like on this course.

Well, maybe a good way to start is to introduce ourselves. I'd like to ask you to form into pairs with people you don't know — or don't know well. So couples can separate for this. Here are some questions to talk about. Please give each person in the group a chance to speak on each question before you move on. After two or three minutes, I'll give you a signal to stop talking and listen to the other person for a few minutes. After a further two or three minutes, we're going to give each of you half a minute to introduce your partner to the rest of the group — who they are, what family they have, why they're doing the course, and what they wouldn't like. Do you understand what's expected, or would you like me to explain again?..

Allow time for each one to speak. This is an important exercise for helping people to relax and for helping the group to bond.

Thanks for doing that exercise — it's to help us begin to feel more comfortable with each other. I hope, during the course, that you'll all move around and sit beside different people each time so that we get to know one another pretty well.

Now you mentioned some things you wouldn't like to happen, so it's important that we set some groundrules right from the beginning to make sure that everyone in the group feels respected and safe. Would you like to look at the groundrules at the back of your book? Other groups have found these useful — and I'd like you to feel free to add to them if you'd like to.

Give out the handbooks, one per person, and allow the group to read the groundrules in silence for a minute or two — but read them aloud if the group has poor reading skills. Encourage comments, and check that they are happy with these rules.

What other ground rules would help to make the course more enjoyable and relaxing and help you to feel safe in the group over the next few weeks?..

There is no fixed charge for this course, so that no one is prevented from doing it, but there are expenses to be met — the cost of the handbooks and of the copy-books, and the cost of training people to run these courses so that many more people can be reached — so there will be an opportunity to donate money at the end of each session, and it's hoped that most of you will be able to put at least (£1) into the 'secret bag' that will be passed around.

At this stage, you could put up a home-made poster, showing the plan of each session.

POSTER   OUTLINE FOR EACH SESSION

    1. How we got on

    2. Tips from the handbook

    3. Music and quietening

    4. Prayer with the New Testament

    5. Feedback and comments

    6. Final details

You can see from this poster how each session works. Maybe I'll just go through each of the six sections.

1. How we got on. Each week, you'll be given some passages to pray on and some tips for prayer, so from next week on, you'll have a chance to talk about how you got on during the week — whether you were plain bored, or delighted, or totally distracted, or whatever.

2. Tips from the handbook. Then we'll move on to the new topic for the week and look at some tips from the handbook you've just received — you're asked to read a few pages of the handbook each week before the meeting.

3. Quietening down. There's a story in the handbook of a child who heard oranges were tasty, and bit into one without peeling it. The point is made that prayer is a bit like that — that we need a chance to quieten down and change gear before we start to pray. So we'll try that, closing our eyes, relaxing and quietening down with a little background music.

4. Prayer with the New Testament. Some people find the Bible boring because they see it as history, thousands of years old. But the Bible is no ordinary book — when the New Testament is read, we believe that Christ is really present, and we hope to experience that for ourselves during these six weeks together. So, as a sign of the presence of Jesus, the light of the world, perhaps I'll light a candle in front of the open Bible now...

5. Feedback and comments. Towards the end of each session, you'll have a chance to talk about how you found the session, what happened for you, or what you liked or disliked, or you can just say in one single word how you're feeling.

6. Final details. And finally, a few details — mainly looking to the week ahead and what we'll do between sessions.

2. Introducing the new topic (10-15 minutes)

I'd ask you now to open your books at the end of chapter one — at the summary of tips..

Read through the tips, sharing personally, where possible, on them — where and when **you** pray, what **you** do, etc.) When you come to the

16

suggestion about using a notebook, give a notebook to each one, for that underlines the fact that you do expect people to write, but you can reassure them that the notebook is private — they will not have to show it to anyone else. Point out that it also makes it much easier for them to talk about what happened for them during the week when they have made a few brief notes each day. When you have introduced the tips, you might ask:

I wonder if there's anything you would like to say about any of these tips, or how you feel personally about using them...

People who have difficulties with any of the suggestions should be respected and helped to see the tips as **options.** Joyce Huggett's book, 'Listening to God' might be recommended as a good example of how someone coming from a low-church tradition learned to appreciate most of these suggestions for herself after having had an initial reaction against them. But it's probably best not to delay on this section; move on quickly to the next section, when the group will have an actual experience of praying.

3. Quietening down (3-4 minutes)

Right, well, we've just seen that it can be useful to begin praying by relaxing and quietening down. So let's try that for a few minutes. I'll put on a little background music to help..

Play music, and dim lights.

This may be the first chance some of you have had all day to quieten down, so it's suggested that you keep your back straight but make yourself comfortable, and take a few slow, deep breaths. Just concentrate on your breathing... (1 minute)

Read slowly, pausing at the continuous dots.

Now become aware of your back touching the back of the chair.. Next, don't move, just feel how your clothes are touching your shoulders — you may feel your shoulders relaxing as you become aware of that.. Next your hands resting in your lap.. Next your bottom on the chair.. Now your feet on the ground — don't move them, just become aware of them.. Again your back.. your shoulders.. your right hand.. your left hand.. your bottom on the chair.. your left foot.. your right foot.. Once again — shoulders, back, and so on. Move around your

body, becoming aware of each part briefly and then on to the next part. Try this for a minute or two...

(The exercise above has been adapted with permission from Anthony de Mello's book 'Sadhana').

4. Praying with the New Testament (20-30 minutes)

We'll move on now to praying with the New Testament

Before I read the passage, which is about the evening of Easter Sunday, I'd like you to close your eyes and imagine what it was like in the upper room where the disciples were.

Change the atmosphere by playing music softly and using the reading light instead of the main light. Read slowly, pausing at the continuous dots.

Imagine the Room

Look at the walls in the upper room — rough, simple walls — can you see the light from the lamps flickering on them?... Now the doors, with big wooden bolts across them that show the fear the disciples have... Put your hand on the rough wood and feel it, even smell it.. Next the disciples — what are they wearing?... See the fear in their eyes — fear that the Jews will come and take them away as they did to their master... Also a little bit of excitement, hardly daring to believe the rumours that Jesus is risen... But mostly fear...

Read the story slowly, pausing at each stroke. John 20 19-21

'It was late that Sunday evening, and the disciples were gathered together behind locked doors/ because they were afraid of the Jewish authorities./ Then Jesus came and stood among them./ 'Peace be with you,' he said./ After saying this, he showed them his hands and his side./ The disciples were filled with joy at seeing the Lord./ Jesus said to them again, 'Peace be with you.'

Now, it may help us to remember that the events described in Scripture can happen here and now for us; the words Jesus speaks are addressed not just to the disciples but to each of us. Jesus is risen. He is alive. He is present here with us now — with great love for each of us. Allow him to enter the room and ask you what the things are that you are most afraid of in your life at present. Then allow him to say to you personally "Peace be with you". Because that is what he really is

18

doing — healing your fears and bringing you a peace that no one can take away.

Read the passage again slowly.

We'll take five or six minutes now to pray in silence. You could put yourself in the upper room, and meet Jesus. Then you may like to repeat a number of times a word or a phrase, like 'Peace be with you,' and let it sink into your heart — or listen to what Jesus wants to say to you. Whatever helps...

After about three minutes, people may begin to lose concentration, so it may help to suggest:

If you find it difficult to keep up a conversation with Jesus, just let him put his hands on your shoulders and say 'Peace be with you;' and you might keep repeating those words over and over again...

A few minutes later:

Before you finish, perhaps you would like to make some little plan from your prayer — we're kind of missing the point, aren't we, if we tell Jesus we love him but we don't make time to love someone who is close to us, perhaps in our own family. To what one person in your family or community will you carry that peace Jesus has just offered you? — maybe tomorrow morning, when everyone is rushing and in bad form. Who will you show love to, and how?... (allow up to two minutes)

We'll end our prayer now by taking a minute more to thank God for all we have been given and to ask for the grace to carry out our plan..

After a minute or so, you could switch off the music, and continue.

5. Feedback and summing up. (about 10 minutes)

Would you like to have a little chat now just for four or five minutes, in threes or fours, about how that went for you. Did you feel like falling asleep, or were you distracted, or what helped you?..

Allow about five minutes or so, longer if necessary.

Thanks for sharing with each other — it's usually enriching to hear how others get on, even to know what their difficulties are. We're

coming now to the end of our first session. This is usually the most difficult session, because we're getting to know one another, and getting used to how the sessions work, so I wouldn't like you to judge the course on this one meeting. But maybe something in the session has confused you — or maybe you're quite pleased to be here — I'd like you to feel free to say what has happened for you during this session or how you're feeling right now at the end of it... Don't be afraid to say what you didn't like, too. So how are you feeling at the end of the session — what did you like, and what were you not so happy with?..

Allow a short period of silence before people talk — it usually takes time for them to gather their thoughts together. If time is running out, you might just ask for a single feeling word from as many as possible — how they are feeling at the end of the session.

6. Concluding remarks. (about 5 minutes)

Read aloud the section introducing the homework, explaining where necessary, and encouraging it as the key to progress in prayer. Also explain where to find the passages in the Bible — be aware that some may not know, for example, what 'MARK 6 30-32' means!

Just before we finish, maybe you'd like to take a minute to have a little chat with the person beside you and decide on a time of the day when you could pray during the week — take a look at the suggestions in the Planning section at the end of chapter two. You see that? And you can write on the line at the end of it what you plan to do..

(Allow about two minutes)

Some people like to know what to expect each session, and that's very simple — the first six chapters correspond to the six topics we'll be covering. So you're asked to read chapter two for next week — as well as chapter one. It's very short, just a few pages, but it does help a lot to have it read. Please bring the handbooks with you to our next meeting. Also the copy-books — you may find that you'll have forgotten what's happened in prayer, so I would remind you to jot down a few lines after each time of prayer about how it went, and to bring your notebook along to the next meeting.

Important to get the 15 mns each day. Its your special time —

20

This is a self-help group, and in keeping with that we ask a different person to take responsibility for a very simple snack at the end of each session. Can we have a volunteer for next week?..

As you might imagine, the key to the success of this course is what you do between sessions. I would encourage you to make sure you get that special fifteen minutes each day. I look forward to meeting you all again next _____ day and hearing how you get on. And please do come back next week, even if you have a hectic week and you don't get a single moment to pray, or if you feel you're getting nowhere! Sometimes people feel discouraged at the beginning — but it's only natural to meet a certain amount of difficulty in learning something new.

So thank you for giving up your time to be here, and for your trust in coming and getting involved. I'll just end by passing around the secret bag, so that you can make some contribution each week to the costs of books and notebooks and the training of people to run these courses.

Pass secret bag.

SESSION TWO

Checklist

Your own handbook;

Your copy-book (with some notes on your week's prayer).

Bible, opened in a central position;

Cassette with suitable instrumental music, and cassette player;

This leader's guide;

Reading light (it can help the atmosphere during sharing and during prayer exercises to switch off the main light and use only a reading light).

Candle and matches;

'Secret bag' for donations;

1. Introduction (about 5 minutes)

We'd like to welcome you all back — thanks for making the effort to come. During these few weeks, you're asked to move around and sit beside different people each time so that we all get to know one another pretty well. I'd ask you, therefore, for this session, to make sure you're sitting beside people you weren't sitting next to last week, preferably people you don't know — or don't know well.

I'll light the candle now in front of the open Bible to remind us that Jesus, the light of the world, is present when the Word of God is read.

Last week you talked about where you come in your family, so maybe now you'd like to have a little chat in pairs or threes, telling a little more about your family — about your children or parents or granny or anyone you like... (about 3 minutes)   *Ⓘ P 55 Part. Manual*

It may be helpful to mention some of the groundrules agreed in the first session, perhaps confidentiality, or the commitment to praying for fifteen minutes per day, particularly if new people have joined the group. For new people, a recap of last week's ideas might also be helpful, perhaps based on the Tips at the end of Chapter One.

2. How we got on. (20-30 minutes)

It may help to ease people into talking if you allow them to chat together in threes first about how they got on with prayer during the week.

Maybe you'd like to form into little groups of three now and take a few minutes to chat about how you got on with praying on the Scripture passages during the week..

After about five minutes, you can then encourage sharing in the larger group. Take some time on the following questions, not dwelling long on any one. But don't be rigid — feel free to skip some of the questions rather than have repetition, particularly if people are talking freely. You will also need to be flexible with the questions if you find that people have not made time for prayer during the previous week — but don't let that discourage you! It is probably a good idea to consult your notebook when talking about your own prayer — that gives others permission to do the same, and provides a model for them. If some have forgotten their notebooks, highlight the importance of writing in them as a help to progressing in prayer, and encourage them to bring them along each week.

We'll take a little time now on how you got on during the week. I'd remind you that you don't have to talk, and that what you say can be as brief as you like — though you will tend to get more out of the course if you do speak.

How about a time for praying — was it difficult to find time, and what times did you find most helpful?...

Then, place — was it difficult to find a quiet place that suited you?.. Did you kneel or sit or squat?

What about getting down to prayer? One suggestion was that you might mark your passage before you started and that you would take time to quieten down, and then ask the Holy Spirit to teach you to pray. What suggestions did you find helpful for getting down to prayer, or was it hard to get started?...

Another suggestion was to begin by noticing God noticing you, perhaps listening to God telling you how much he loves you — how fond he is of you. Did you try that, or was it difficult?...

It was suggested that you would use your notebook to cope with distractions and to write up your prayer briefly afterwards, I wonder if that was helpful?...

Then the actual prayer itself. I wonder if you found the passages hard to pray on, or what difficulties or distractions you experienced, or how you felt in general during prayer — bored, excited, distracted, warm, peaceful, dry, or whatever? In sharing these things, negative and positive, your honesty can be a great help to everyone else in the group...

This is an important part of each session. Don't be afraid of silence — it may take a little while for people to get their thoughts together and to warm up. But it is good to be willing to chip in yourself and say how things went for you — just don't be too perfect! And don't worry if little appears to have happened in the first week — it all takes time.

3. Introducing the new topic (5-10 minutes) *End of Chap 2 p. 68*

Ask everyone to open their books at the end of chapter two — at the summary of tips. Unless people have poor reading skills, you might allow a minute or so for them to read the tips for themselves. You might introduce this section something like this:

I hope you all got a chance to read chapter two. It's about Jesus of Nazareth, the person we meet in prayer. Last week, it was suggested that we begin our prayer by just noticing God noticing us. But if I see God as frightening, or if I feel mostly guilty in God's presence, then my prayer is going to be off balance, isn't it? That's why we need to pray for a truer understanding of who Jesus is as a loving and forgiving friend — and that is a grace that he dearly wants to give us as we work at changing our false notions. Now, there's a summary of the tips from chapter two at the end of the chapter, and you might like to take a minute or so to read those tips.

After a minute or two:

I wonder was there anything new for you in chapter two, or how you found it — or if you have any comments on these tips?...

Encourage comments rather than questions, not by teaching, but by

25

showing an openness to people's experience. So you might answer questions with: 'I wonder what does anyone else think about this, or what's your experience of it?' You might also make a few comments from your own experience on any of the tips. Teach by sharing — not by preaching. It's probably best not to delay on this section, but to move on quickly to the next section when they will have an actual experience of praying.

4. Quietening down (5-10 minutes)

We'll move on to praying now, and we'll begin this section, as usual, by relaxing and quietening down. We saw that this is useful before prayer, but its value is even being recognised now in hospitals, where people are actually learning meditation and quietening exercises to prevent heart disease!

Play music, and dim lights.

We'll take body awareness first, as we did last week, and I'll put on a little background music to help.. (Music)

Now, become aware of your feet on the ground — don't move them, just become aware of them.. next, your right foot.. your left foot.. your bottom on the chair.. now, your hands resting in your lap.. your right hand.. your left hand.. your back touching the back of the chair.. your clothes touching your shoulders — you may feel your shoulders relaxing as you become aware of that..

Once again, your feet on the ground — your right foot.. your left foot.. your bottom on the chair.. your hands resting in your lap.. your right hand.. your left hand.. your back touching the back of the chair.. your clothes touching your shoulders..

And again, feet, bottom, hands, back, and so on, move around your body, becoming aware of each part briefly and then on to the next part. Try this for a minute or two... (About 2 minutes).

Next, become aware of your breathing. Just continue breathing as you have been, but notice the cool air as it enters your nose, and the warm air as it passes out. Be peaceful, let yourself relax, and continue noticing your breathing for a minute or two. Any thoughts that come to you, just put them aside and keep concentrating on breathing in and out... (About 2 minutes)

26

5. Praying with the New Testament (20-30 minutes)

We'll move on now to praying with Scripture.

In this session, we're looking at the importance of meeting Jesus in prayer. We join the blind man, Bartimaeus, as he sits beside the road out of Jericho. When he was cured and his eyes were opened, the first thing he saw was Jesus. So we might do well to put ourselves in Bartimaeus' shoes and pray that our blindness will also be healed so that we too may see Jesus as he really is — a good friend who cares deeply about each of us personally, and wishes us really well.

We notice too that Bartimaeus liked the Jesus he saw, for St Mark tells us that, when he was cured, he then followed Jesus, so it's a great example of what we go to prayer for — to see Jesus more clearly, love him more dearly, and follow him more nearly. As I read the story slowly now, you might come with your own blindness to Jesus and let him say or do to you what he says and does to the blind man.

Change the atmosphere by using a reading light instead of the main light. Then read the passage slowly, pausing at all natural breaks. Mark 10 46-52.

They came to Jericho., and as Jesus was leaving with his disciples and a large crowd, a blind beggar named Bartimaeus son of Timaeus was sitting by the road./ When he heard that it was Jesus of Nazareth, he began to shout, "Jesus! Son of David! Take pity on me!"/ Many of the people scolded him and told him to be quiet./ But he shouted even more loudly./ "Son of David, take pity on me!"/ Jesus stopped and said "Call him."/ So they called the blind man. "Cheer up!" they said. "Get up, he is calling you."/ He threw off his cloak, jumped up and came to Jesus./ "What do you want me to do for you?" Jesus asked him./ "Teacher," the blind man answered, "I want to see again."/ "Go," Jesus told him, "your faith has made you well,"/ At once he was able to see/ and he followed Jesus on the road.

Would you like to read down through the story on your own now — it's at the end of chapter two, and maybe you'd pick out one word or phrase that strikes you? Don't say why it strikes you — just say the word or phrase aloud..

When everyone has spoken, continue:

I'll play some music now and give you five or six minutes for prayer, perhaps on any of the phrases you have just heard.
The words Jesus speaks are addressed not just to Bartimaeus but to each of us. He is present here with us now — with great love for each of us. Let him ask you, as he asked Bartimaeus, 'What do you want?' and let him speak to you personally. Because that's what he wants to do..

Play music, and change the atmosphere by using the reading light instead of the main light. Five or six minutes may seem short, but remember that that is a long time for people who are not used to prayer. Better to whet their appetites than to leave them bored. After a few minutes, indeed, they may lose concentration, so it may help to say:

As you continue talking and listening to Jesus, it may help to answer the question Jesus asks you today "What do you want me to do for you?...

After a further two or three minutes:

In this passage, we are meeting Jesus, and being invited to follow him. So in what way can we follow Jesus over the next twenty-four hours — when we are with our families or friends, at home, or in the street, or anywhere? It's usually a good idea to end our prayer by making some practical little plan so that we'll be different as a result of praying.

After another minute or two:

And we'll end our prayer now as usual by taking a minute more to thank God for all we have been given and to ask for the grace to carry out any plan we may have made.

After a minute or so, you could switch off the music and continue.

6. Feedback and summing up (about 10 minutes)

Would you like to have a little chat now just for four or five minutes, in threes or fours, about how that went for you. — even if you felt bored or completely distracted. You could talk about what helped you and what didn't help, and how you felt..

Allow about five minutes or so, longer if necessary.

Thanks for sharing with each other — it's usually enriching to hear how others get on, even to know what their difficulties are. We're coming now to the end of our session. We've been trying to clear the lines of communication and meet the real Jesus of Nazareth. So I'd like you to feel free to say just how you're feeling right now at the end of this session together... You might mention how your prayer went, or what you liked about the session, or what you weren't so happy about — just whatever you'd like to say, or how you're feeling at the end of it...

Allow a short period of silence before people talk — it usually takes time for them to gather their thoughts together. If time is running out, you might just ask for a single feeling word from as many as possible — how they are feeling at the end of the session.

7. Concluding remarks

Just before we finish, maybe you'd like to take a minute to have a little chat with the person beside you and decide where might be the best place for you to pray — take a look at the suggestions in the Planning section at the end of chapter two. And you can write on the line at the end of it what you plan to do..

(Allow about two minutes)

As we come to the end of our session, I'd just like to highlight the passages for the coming week (at the end of chapter two).

If you think it necessary, explain what they are being asked — to do over the next week.

I can't emphasise enough the importance of making the time to pray on these passages between sessions — that's the key to progress. No one can teach you to pray except the Holy Spirit — so you have to learn by practising. I would encourage you all to make sure to get that special fifteen minutes each day. It may seem like a big commitment, but it's so worthwhile. And also to use your copy-book to jot down a few lines after each time of prayer about how it went, and to bring it along to the next meeting. I look forward to meeting you all again next

_____ day and hearing how you get on. You're also asked to read chapter three during the coming week — again, it's quite short, but it will help a lot to have it read before the next session.

Before I pass around the 'secret bag,' can we have a volunteer to bring the snack next week?..

Pass the secret bag.

Well, that's the end of our session. Thank you very much for giving up your time to be here, and for the trust you've shown.

SESSION THREE

Checklist

Your handbook;

Your copy-book (with some notes on your week's prayer);

Bible, opened in a central position;

Cassette with suitable instrumental music, and cassette player;

This leader's guide;

Reading light (it can help the atmosphere during sharing and during prayer exercises to switch off the main light and use only a reading light);

Candle and matches;

'Secret bag' for donations;

1. Introduction (about 5 minutes)

(1) Welcome, everyone — and thanks for making the effort to come. In the last session we tried to form a clearer picture of Jesus, and this week, our concentration is on forming a more real picture of who we are ourselves in relation to God. *know each other - who again*

(2) I'd ask you, as usual, to make sure you're sitting beside people you weren't sitting next to before.

(3) I'll light the candle now in front of the open Bible to remind us that we're not praying on our own — we're joining in with the whole people of God in the continuous prayer of Jesus to the Father.

Last week we began by getting to know each other a little better, talking about where we come in our families. So maybe now we'll just concentrate on the names. The first person says 'I'm (John).' The next says 'I'm (Joanne) and this is (John).' Next 'I'm (Barbara) and this is (Joanne) and this is (John)...

Would you like to try that, and we'll see how far we get.. (3-5 mins)

(X) It may be helpful to mention one or two of the groundrules agreed in the first session, especially if you feel that one of them is being ignored.

31

2. How we got on (20-30 minutes)

If the group is a quiet one, feel free to give them a few minutes first to chat in threes about how they got on during the week.

We'll move on now to take a little time on how you got on during the week. If you want to check your notebook, that may help to jog your memory. I'd remind you that you don't have to talk, and that what you say can be as brief as you like — though you will tend to get more out of the course if you do speak.

You can mention anything you like — for example, what time or place have you found useful for praying? How did you get on in quietening down or getting into prayer? Was it hard to imagine God loving you? Did you find it helpful to use the notebook? Then the actual prayer itself. I wonder if you found the passages hard to pray on; or what difficulties or distractions you experienced; or how you felt during prayer — did you have a sense of meeting Jesus? What stood out for you or surprised you? Were you real with God? In sharing these things, negative and positive, your honesty can be a great help to others...

This is an important section. Don't be afraid of silence — it may take a little while for people to get their thoughts together and to warm up. But it is good to be willing to chip in yourself and say how things went for you. You may need to say a few words of encouragement at the end, pointing out that it takes time to feel comfortable with any new skills or methods — you might remind them of how awkward it felt when they were beginning to learn to ride a bicycle, but how soon they became skilled.

3. Introducing the new topic (5-10 minutes)

Last week, we began to look at how we see God, and especially how we see Jesus. We saw that a wrong picture of God can handicap us in prayer. But there's another thing that can handicap us — and that is if we have a wrong picture of ourselves. God made us good — that's on the very first page of the Bible — God loves us, and is delighted with us. Now obviously it would be spiritual pride to take the credit myself for my goodness and virtues, but it can be equally wrong

to deny them; this false notion that it's wrong to recognise my goodness and the virtues God gave me doesn't make sense, for how can I love others if I don't believe in myself and my own goodness?

The point is also made in the chapter that we are all sinners, and that we need to pray for the grace of a deeper sense of sin in our lives, but too much emphasis on that shows a lack of trust in God who is forgiveness itself. So I am a sinner, yes — but I'm very much a loved sinner, and as soon as I turn to God repentant, I am forgiven.

Now, I hope you all got a chance to read chapter three — there's a summary of the tips from it at the end of the chapter, and you might like to take a minute or so to read it.

Ask everyone to open their books at the end of chapter three — at the summary of tips. Unless people have poor reading skills, you might allow a minute or so for them to read the tips for themselves. Allow time for reading the tips.

After a minute or two:

I wonder if there was anything new for you in chapter three, or how you found it — or if you would like to comment on any of the tips?..

Again, feel free to allow people to chat together in groups of three, if you feel that would be more appropriate. Encourage comments rather than questions, not by teaching, but by showing an openness to people's experience. So you might answer questions with: 'I wonder what does anyone else think about this, or what's your experience of it?' You might also feel free to make a few comments from your own experience on any of the tips. Teach by sharing rather than by preaching. It's probably best not to delay on this section, but to move on quickly to the next section when they will have an actual experience of praying.

4. Quietening down (about 6-7 minutes)

As usual, we'll begin our prayer by relaxing and quietening down. Some writers on prayer say that it's okay to spend our entire prayer time calming down and finding silence inside ourselves because they claim that it is only in that silence that we can truly meet God.

I'll put on a little background music to help..

Play music and use the reading light instead of the main light.

Now, become aware of your breathing. As you do, you might breathe a little deeper and more slowly. Notice the cool air as it enters your nose, and the warm air as it passes out. Keep your back fairly straight, but be peaceful, and relax, and notice your breathing for a few minutes. Any thoughts that come to you, just put them aside and keep concentrating on breathing in and out... (About two minutes)

As you breathe in, you could say something like the name 'Jesus' — that may help you to meet him — or 'Come, Holy Spirit' or 'Come, Lord Jesus' — whatever phrase appeals to you, and become aware of the presence of God within you, noticing you, loving you...

As you breathe out each time, it may help to hand over to God all your pressures, your guilt, your worries..

(Another three minutes, approximately)

5. Praying with the New Testament (20-30 minutes)

We'll move on now to praying with the New Testament. One of the benefits of doing a scripture-based course on prayer is how it renews passages which we have become over-familiar with. We're going to look at the story of the prodigal son, and we chose this passage because it's a good illustration of what we've been talking about. The focus is not so much on the sinner as on the father. What is often overlooked is that the poor man has lost both sons — the elder brother has no real relationship with his father at all. For years he has done all the right things — but with the wrong attitude "For years," he says, "I have worked for you like a slave." His father isn't seen as a father but as a slave master. Sadly, many of us tend to see God like that, we'll do all our duties, but out of a sense of duty, not for love. The elder brother won't even recognise his brother as brother — "this son of yours" he calls him, for he looks down on him. Jesus often pointed out that it's the respectable people who think they're better and who judge others, who are the great sinners. Can you imagine how hurtful it must be to the father when we are like the elder brother? If you were the father of

34

a teenage son who treated you like that, you would probably be so angry. Yet this forgiving old man who has lost both his sons opens his hands to his angry son and says "All I have is yours." He is the important person in the story of the Prodigal Son. We need to focus, not so much on ourselves as sinners, but on this loving father and how we have hurt him, and how he keeps opening his arms, forgiving, saying "All I have is yours." As I read the story, you could close your eyes and put yourself into it — speak to the father, repentant and let the father speak to you and love you and forgive you.

Change the atmosphere by playing music and using the reading light instead of the main light. Read the section of the story from verses 17-32 of Luke 15.

At last he came to his senses and said,/ 'All my father's hired workers have more than they can eat, and here I am about to starve!/ I will get up and go to my father and say, Father, I have sinned against God and against you./ I am no longer fit to be called your son.'/ So he got up and started back to his father.

He was still a long way from home when his father saw him;/ his heart was filled with pity, and he ran, threw his arms round his son, and kissed him./ "Father," the son said, "I have sinned against God and against you. I am no longer fit to be called your son."/ But the father called his servants. "Hurry!" he said. "Bring the best robe and put it on him. Put a ring on his finger and shoes on his feet. Then go and get the prize calf and kill it, and let us celebrate with a feast!/ For this son of mine was dead, but now he is alive, he was lost, but now he has been found." And so the feasting began./ In the meantime the elder son was out in the field. On his way back, when he came close to the house, he heard the music and dancing. So he called one of the servants and asked him, "What's going on?" "Your brother has come back home," the servant answered, "and your father has killed the prize calf, because he got him back safe and sound."/ The elder brother was so angry that he would not go into the house,/ so his father came out and begged him to come in./ But he answered his father, "Look, all these years I have worked for you like a slave,/ and

I have never disobeyed your orders./ What have you given me? Not even a goat for me to have a feast with my friends!/ But this son of yours wasted all your property on prostitutes, and when he comes back home, you kill the prize calf for him!''/ "My son," the father answered, "you are always here with me and everything I have is yours./ But we had to celebrate and be happy, because your brother was dead, but now he is alive;/ he was lost, but now he has been found."

Would you like to look at the passage now and pick out one word or phrase that strikes you. Don't say why it strikes you — just say the word or phrase aloud.. (Allow time).

I'll play some music now and give you five or six minutes for prayer, just talking and listening to this sad, vulnerable, father who has no bitterness — or even just watching him come hurrying down the road to meet you.

After three or four minutes, it may help concentration to suggest:

I would just mention that you may like to confess your sin to the father and experience how deeply and totally he forgives you and loves you.

After another two or three minutes:

This passage is also about the way we treat each other in our family, and how we can forgive and be reconciled, so maybe now we can look ahead over the next 24 hours and make some practical little plan, especially about someone you need to forgive or ask forgiveness of..

After another minute or two

And we'll end our prayer now as usual by taking a minute more to thank God for all we have been given and to ask for the grace to carry out any plan we may have made.

Depending on what time is available, you might encourage anyone who wishes to make a prayer aloud:

Maybe we'll just take a minute or two for as many of you as possible to make some little prayer aloud — something arising from your prayer or any needs you're aware of, for our prayers are specially powerful when we pray together with Jesus in our midst.

36

Bear in mind, however, that it is not fair to keep people late. Leave enough time for the final sharing.

6. Summing up and comments (5-10 minutes)

Would you like to share now with two or three others how your prayer went? You could talk about what helped your prayer or what made it difficult, how you felt, or how you got on..

Allow about five minutes for this chat — depending on how relaxed and open they are with each other. Then:

We're coming now to the end of the session. We've been trying to clear the lines of communication and see more clearly who we are as we come to God. So I'd like you to feel free to say just how you're feeling right now at the end of this session together... You might mention how your prayer went, or what you liked about the session, or what you weren't so happy about — just whatever you'd like to say, or how you're feeling at the end of the session...

Allow a short period of silence before people talk — it usually takes time for them to gather their thoughts together.

7. Concluding remarks

Just before we finish, maybe you'd like to take a minute to have a little chat with the person beside you and decide on some gestures or positions you might experiment with for prayer — take a look at the suggestions in the Planning section at the end of chapter three. And you can write on the line at the end of it what you plan to do..

(Allow about two minutes)

As we come to the end of our session, I'd like to highlight the passages for the coming week (at the end of chapter three).

If you think it necessary, explain what they are being asked to do over the next week.

I can't emphasise enough the importance of making the time to pray on these passages between sessions — that's the key to progress. I would encourage you all to make sure you get that special fifteen minutes each day. I look forward to meeting you all again next _____

day and hearing how you get on. You're also asked to read chapter four during the coming week — again, it's quite short, but it will help a lot to have it read before the next session. And also to use your copybook to jot down a few lines after each time of prayer about how it went, and to bring your notes along with you to the next meeting.

Before I pass around the 'secret bag,' can we have a volunteer to bring the snack next week?..

Pass the secret bag.

Well, that's the end of our session. Thank you very much for giving up your time to be here, and for the trust you've shown.

SESSION FOUR

Checklist

Your handbook:

Your copy-book (with some notes on your week's prayer);

Bible, opened in a central position;

Cassette with suitable instrumental music, and cassette player;

This leader's guide;

Reading light (it can help the atmosphere during sharing and during prayer exercises to switch off the main light and use only a reading light);

Candle and matches;

'Secret bag' for donations;

1. Introduction (about 5 minutes)

Welcome, everyone — and thanks for making the effort to come. In the last few sessions we've been trying to clear the lines of communication to form a clearer picture of who God is and who we are. This week, we move on to look at how we can listen better to God in prayer.

I'd ask you, as usual, to make sure you're sitting beside people you weren't sitting next to last week... Maybe you'd tell the person beside you one thing that happened last week that you'd like to thank God for.

I'll light the candle now in front of the open Bible to remind us of the presence of Jesus, the light of the world, as we read the Word of God.

It may be helpful to mention one or two of the groundrules agreed in the first session, especially if you feel that one of them is being ignored. Or you could highlight the importance of writing in the notebook.

2. How we got on (20-30 minutes)

If the group is a quiet one, feel free to give them a few minutes first to chat in threes about how they got on during the week.

We'll move on now to take a little time on how you got on during the week. I'd remind you that you don't have to talk, and that what you say can be as brief as you like — though you will tend to get more out of the course if you do speak.

You can mention anything you like — what you found helpful in terms of time or place, or quietening down, or becoming aware of the presence of God. You could mention how you got on with any of the passages, and whether you had a sense of meeting Jesus and being real with him, and what stood out for you or surprised you. I'd just remind you that in talking about your prayer and in writing about your prayer each day, we are asked to write our own personal reactions and our feelings. We've seen that this is not a scripture study group — the emphasis is not on your understanding of the scripture passage, but on what it's saying to you personally, how you felt, and how you got on, including perhaps any difficulties you experienced in praying. So you're encouraged to speak personally and honestly, and to be as brief as you like. Just a few of the more important points rather than a blow by blow account of the week...

If there has not been a problem with someone overtalking at the previous session, there is no need to set time limits, especially since there will be occasions when some people may **need** longer to talk.

This is an important section of each session. Don't be afraid of silence — it may take a little while for people to get their thoughts together and to warm up. But it is good to be willing to chip in yourself and say how things went for you, including any difficulties or surprises you experienced. Don't go beyond about 30 minutes on this section, or the rest of the session may suffer.

3. Introducing the new topic (5-10 minutes)

We'll move on now to the topic for this session. As you know, only God can teach you to pray, but God usually works through human methods; God's grace normally builds on nature. So the purpose of this course is to learn and to practise better communication methods in prayer — to help to open the communication lines that allow God's

40

grace through. We started by looking at how we can prepare better for meeting God in prayer — some suggestions on getting down to prayer and preparing to meet a good friend — then we looked at how we might develop a truer picture of a loving God and of myself as a forgiven sinner, because all these are essential for clearing the lines of communication. Now we move on to a very important communication skill — learning to listen better to God.

I hope you all got a chance to read chapter four — there's a summary of the tips from it at the end of the chapter, and you might like to take a minute or so to read them.

Ask everyone to open their books at the end of chapter four — at the summary of tips. Unless people have poor reading skills, you might allow a minute or so for them to read the tips for themselves. Allow time for reading the tips.

After a minute or two:

I wonder if there was anything new for you in chapter four, or how you found it — or if you would like to comment on any of these tips?..

Encourage comments rather than questions, not by teaching, but by showing an openness to people's experience. So you might answer questions with: 'I wonder what does anyone else think about this, or what's your experience of it?' You might also feel free to make a few comments from your own experience on any of the tips. It's probably best not to delay on this section, but to move on quickly to the next section when they will have an actual experience of praying.

4. Quietening down (about 6-7 minutes)

As usual, we'll begin our prayer by relaxing and quietening down. We saw it can be useful to begin prayer by relaxing and calming down. Different things help different people to relax — if something puts you to sleep, or doesn't help you to get into prayer, you'll have to experiment until you find what does help you most. I'll put on a little background music to help..

Play music, and dim lights.

41

Now, become aware of your breathing. As you do, you might breathe a little deeper and more slowly. Notice the cool air as it enters your nose, and the warm air as it passes out. Keep your back fairly straight, but be peaceful, and relax, and notice your breathing for a few minutes. Any thoughts that come to you, just put them aside and keep concentrating on breathing in and out... (About three minutes)

As you breathe in, you could say something like the name 'Jesus' — that may help you to meet him — or 'Come, Holy Spirit' or 'Come, Lord Jesus' or 'Lord, teach us to pray — whatever phrase appeals to you...

As you breathe in that prayer, become aware of the presence of God within you, noticing you, loving you, teaching you to pray...

As you breathe out each time, you might hand over to God your life, your pressures, your guilt, your worries..

5. Praying with the New Testament (20-30 minutes)

We'll move on now to praying with the New Testament, and I'd like to begin by describing the scene. I'll put on some background music first.. *Read this w/es Passage together*

Dim the lights and play instrumental music quietly. As you read the following passage, go very slowly, pausing each time at the continuous dots.

You can begin by just relaxing. Close your eyes, or whatever helps you to relax, and imagine the scene..

You are in the Holy Land. It's spring time... Spring comes early, so it's quite warm... Notice the hills in the distance... Fields... A man walking up and down one field, scattering seed — it's a lovely picture.. Now look at the lake — a huge lake, it's more like a sea.. Next, look at the hundreds of people standing on the beach. Country people mostly. Look at their wrinkled faces... What expressions do you see?.. Some are curious, some excited — they've come to see a miracle or some wonder. Some are disbelieving.. See the group of pharisees at the side. Some of them are interested enough, but most of them are threatened and hostile — there to find fault.. Now the fishing boat that Jesus gets

42

into to speak to them... What is he wearing?.. Look at his feet, sweaty and dusty from the heat.. See his hands now — not perfect, smooth hands — let him be human. Hands that have been used to hard work, maybe a broken fingernail... Now look at his face. Serious, but there's warmth and compassion in the eyes.. Look at his eyes as he looks at you.. Hear him say your name.. Now listen to him speak to you as he tells you this story..

Read the parable of the sower, Luke 8, verses 5-8 and 11-15.

Once there was a man who went out to sow corn./ As he scattered the seed in the field, some of it fell along the path, where it was stepped on and the birds ate it up./ Some of it fell on rocky ground and when the plants sprouted, they dried up because the soil had no moisture./ Some of the seed fell among thorn bushes which grew up with the plants and choked them./ And some seeds fell in good soil; the plants grew and produced corn a hundred grains each./ Listen, then, if you have ears!/ This is what the parable means; the seed is the word of God./ The seeds that fell along the path stand for those who hear, but the Devil comes and takes the message away from their hearts in order to keep them from believing and being saved./ The seeds that fell on rocky ground stand for those who hear the message and receive it gladly. But it does not sink deep into them. They believe only for a while, but when the time of testing comes, they fall away./ The seeds that fell among thorn bushes stand for those who hear, but the worries and riches and pleasures of this life crowd in and choke them, and their fruit never ripens./ The seeds that fell in good soil stand for those who hear the message and retain it in a good and obedient heart, and they persist until they bear fruit.

Maybe you'd like to look at the passage in your book now, pick out a word or phrase that strikes you, and say it aloud..

When everyone has spoken:

I'll play some music now and we'll take five or six minutes to pray in silence. We suggest that you try any of the suggestions for praying. Either picture Jesus and let him continue talking to you, or take one of the words or phrases you've just heard, and repeat it slowly, allowing it to sink into your heart.

For those whose concentration is poor, it can help to add a further suggestion after about three minutes:

It may help to allow Jesus to ask you how open and receptive you are to the seed he is sowing in you — even how open you want to be — and to tell him what your fears are.

After a few minutes more:

As we pray each day, it is recommended that we end by making a practical plan. When we listen deeply to God, he's usually asking us, not to pray more, but to love more — which is the sign of a disciple of Jesus. And for most of us, that means loving more in our own family. In this passage, Jesus asks us to listen if we have ears to hear, so which person in my family do I need to hold my tongue with in order to listen better to them..

After another minute or two

And we'll end our prayer now as usual by taking a minute more to thank God for all we have been given and to ask for the grace to carry out any plan we may have made.

Depending on what time is available, you might encourage anyone who wishes to make a prayer aloud:

Maybe we'll just take a minute or two for as many of you as possible to make some little prayer aloud — something arising from your prayer or any needs you're aware of, or any blessings you have received.

Bear in mind, however, that it is not fair to keep people late. Leave enough time for the final sharing.

6. Summing up and comments (5-10 minutes)

Would you like to share now with two or three others how your prayer went?..

Allow about five minutes for this chat — depending on how relaxed and open they are with each other.

We're coming now to the end of this session. We've been looking at how we can listen better in prayer. So I'd like you to feel free to say

just how you're feeling right now at the end of this session together... You might mention how your prayer went, or what you liked about this session, or what you weren't so happy about — just whatever you'd like to say, or how you're feeling at the end of the session...

Allow a short period of silence before people talk — it usually takes time for them to gather their thoughts together.

7. Concluding remarks

Just before we finish, maybe you'd like to take a minute to have a little chat with the person beside you and decide on some symbol or object that you might keep in your prayer place — take a look at the suggestions in the Planning section at the end of chapter four. And you can write on the line at the end of it what you plan to do...

(Allow about two minutes)

As we come to the end of our session, I'd just like to highlight the passages for the coming week, at the end of chapter five. You can always go back over the passage we've been praying on in this session, but the main suggestion for the week ahead is to pray on the first two chapters of Luke's gospel, perhaps listening to the different characters tell you in their own words what happened and how they feel — Mary, Joseph, the shepherds, Simeon, and so on. Just take one scene at a time, but don't feel you have to get through the whole two chapters — stay on any one passage for as long as it helps you..

I can't emphasise enough the importance of making the time to pray on these passages between sessions — that's the key to progress. I would encourage you all to make sure you get that special fifteen minutes each day. I look forward to meeting you all again next _____ day and hearing how you get on. You're also asked to read chapter five during the coming week — again, it's quite short, but it will help a lot to have it read before the next session.

Before I pass around the 'secret bag,' can we have a volunteer to bring the snack next week?..

Pass the secret bag.

Well, that's the end of our session. Thank you very much for giving up your time to be here, and for the trust you've shown.

45

SESSION FIVE

Checklist

Your handbook;

Your copy-book (with some notes on your week's prayer);

Bible, opened in a central position;

Cassette with suitable instrumental music, and cassette player;

This leader's guide;

Reading light (it can help the atmosphere during sharing and during prayer exercises to switch off the main light and use only a reading light);

Candle and matches;

'Secret bag' for donations;

1. Introduction

Welcome, everyone — and thanks for making the effort to come. Last week, we looked at how we can listen better to God in prayer, and this week we'll be looking at how we can talk more from the heart.

I'd ask you, as usual, to make sure you're sitting beside people you weren't sitting next to in the past few weeks.

I'll light the candle now in front of the open Bible to remind us that we're not praying on our own — we're joining in with the whole people of God in the continuous prayer of Jesus to the Father.

2. How we got on (20-30 minutes)

If the group is a quiet one, feel free to give them a few minutes first to chat in threes about how they got on during the week.

We'll move on now to take a little time on how you got on during the week. I'd remind you that you don't have to talk, and that what you say can be as brief as you like — though you will tend to get more out of the course if you do speak.

You can mention anything you like — what you found helpful in terms of time or place to pray, or quietening down, or becoming aware of the presence of God. **You could mention how you got on with any of the passages, and whether you had a sense of meeting Jesus, and what stood out for you or surprised you. Last week, there were various suggestions for listening, like imagining the scene, or letting one of the characters speak, or finding a word or phrase and repeating it — I wonder if some of you found any of these methods helpful during the week. You might just mention a few of the more important points rather than a blow by blow account of the week...**

This is an important section of each session. Don't be afraid of silence — it may take a little while for people to get their thoughts together and to warm up. As usual, it can be helpful if the team also talk about their own prayer and about what is going on in their lives. That is especially useful if people are wandering off the subject and the sharing needs to be brought back on focus. Don't talk for long — remember that your goal is to enable the others. Don't go beyond about 30 minutes on this section, or the rest of the session may suffer.

3. Introducing the new topic (5-10 minutes)

We'll move on now to the topic for this session, which is talking more from the heart in prayer. I hope you all got a chance to read chapter five — it's about ways of making our prayer more real, linking it in with whatever is going on in our daily lives, with our difficulties, our work, the tensions in our families and with others. There's a summary of the tips from it at the end of the chapter, and you might like to take a minute or so to read them.

Ask everyone to open their books at the end of chapter four — at the summary of tips. Unless people have poor reading skills, you might allow a minute or so for them to read the tips for themselves.

After a minute or two:

I wonder if you'd like to mention anything that struck you in chapter five — or if you'd like to comment on any of these tips?..

Encourage comments rather than questions, not by teaching, but by showing an openness to people's experience. So you might answer questions with: 'I wonder what does anyone else think about this, or what's your experience of it?' You might also feel free to make a few comments from your own experience on any of the tips. It's probably best not to delay on this section, but to move on quickly to the next section when they will have an actual experience of praying.

4. Quietening down (about 6-7 minutes)

As usual, we'll begin our prayer by relaxing and quietening down. I'll put on a little background music to help..

Play music, and dim lights.

Now, become aware of your breathing, just continuing to breathe as you have been, or, if you prefer, taking deeper, slower breaths. Keep your back fairly straight, but be peaceful, and relax, and notice your breathing. Any thoughts that come to you; just put them aside and keep concentrating on breathing in and out. Notice the cool air as it enters your nose, and the warm air as it passes out ... (About three minutes)

As you breathe in, you could say something like the name 'Jesus' — that may help you to meet him — or 'Come, Holy Spirit' or 'Come, Lord Jesus' — whatever phrase appeals to you... As you make that prayer, slowly breathe in your deepest longings and desires which God so dearly wants to give you, and become aware of the presence of God within you...

As you breathe out each time, you might hand over to God your life, your pressures, your guilt, your worries...

5. Praying with the New Testament (20-30 minutes)

We'll move on now to praying with the New Testament. Before reading the story, which is about the calming of the storm, we'll just relax and take a little quiet time to become aware of what the storms in our own lives are... What is it that frightens me or makes me lose my peace of mind? Maybe a difficult relationship with a teenager — or with any child.. or with a neighbour, an in-law, a husband or wife.. Or it may be a worry about someone — or a worry about money, or it

49

may be the way work takes over. Or an addiction in my life —
something that overpowers me. We all have our storms that threaten to
destroy us...

Dim the lights, play instrumental music quietly, and pause for a minute
or two.

**Maybe you'd like to take a minute to mention to the person beside
you what one or two of the storms in your life are at present. If it's
something very personal, feel free to pass and not to talk about it, but
it usually helps when we share with others about the crosses and
worries in our lives...**

Allow a few minutes for this sharing.

And with that in mind, we'll listen now to the passage:

Read slowly the story of the storm at sea, Mark 4 35-41.

**On the evening of that same day Jesus said to his disciples, "Let us
go across to the other side of the lake."/ So they left the crowd; the
disciples got into the boat in which Jesus was already sitting and they
took him with them./ Other boats were there too. Suddenly a strong
wind blew up and the waves began to spill over into the boat, so that it
was about to fill with water./ Jesus was in the back of the boat,
sleeping with his head on a pillow./ The disciples woke him up and
said, "Teacher, don't you care that we are about to die?"/ Jesus stood
up and commanded the wind, "Be quiet!"/ and he said to the waves,
"Be still!"/ The wind died down, and there was a great calm./ Then
Jesus said to his disciples, "Why are you frightened? Have you still no
faith?"/ But they were terribly afraid and said to one another, "Who
is this man?/ Even the wind and the waves obey him!"** _P. 40_

**Maybe you'd like to take a minute to read through the passage in
your book now, pick out a word or phrase that strikes you, and say it
aloud..**

When everyone has spoken:

**Now, bearing in mind that what is described in the New Testament
is happening now, that Jesus is really present when the New Testament
is read, calming our storms, bringing peace into our hearts and our
marriages and our family life and our relationships, you could take five**

or six minutes to pray in silence. Try any of the suggestions for talking or listening. Either picture Jesus, and meet him, and let him say these words to you. Or take one of the words or phrases you've just heard, and repeat it over and over slowly, perhaps breathing it in and allowing it to sink into your heart. Or join the disciples in their fear and tell Jesus honestly how you feel about the storms in your life, and listen in your heart to what he says to you. Whatever helps — just be honest and real in your prayer.

After a few minutes it may help concentration to suggest:

We can easily be overcome by the difficulties in our lives when we lose sight of the presence of Jesus, as the disciples did, so I would just remind you, as we continue to pray, of the presence and power of Jesus with us now. You may like to repeat over and over again Jesus' words to you: 'Be quiet. Be still.'

After about two minutes:

Finally, as usual, a practical little plan to end the prayer, opening ourselves up to letting Jesus work through us in our daily lives. We might ask ourselves what part Jesus expects us to play to calm both the storms in ourselves and the storms being experienced by our family and friends. We can plan what we might do, and open ourselves up to Jesus working through us.

After about two minutes:

And we'll end our prayer now as usual by taking a minute more to thank God for all we have been given and to ask for the grace to carry out any plan we may have made.

Depending on what time is available, you might encourage anyone who wishes to make a prayer aloud:

Feel free now, anyone who wishes, to make a little prayer aloud — maybe a word of thanks or something arising out of your prayer..

6. Summing up and comments (5-10 minutes)

Would you like to share now with two or three others how your prayer went — just share whatever you're comfortable with...

Allow about five minutes for this chat — depending on how relaxed and open they are with each other.

We're coming now to the end of this session. We've been looking at how we can listen better in prayer. So I'd like you to feel free to say just how you're feeling right now at the end of this session together... You might mention how your prayer went or what you liked about this session, or what you weren't so happy about — just whatever you'd like to say or how you're feeling at the end of the session...

Allow a short period of silence before people talk — it usually takes time for them to gather their thoughts together.

7. Concluding remarks

Just before we finish, maybe you'd like to take a minute to have a little chat with the person beside you and decide on some ways of keeping in touch with God during the day and carrying your prayer more into your day — take a look at the suggestions in the Planning section at the end of chapter five. And you can write on the line at the end of it what you plan to do...

(Allow about two minutes)

As we come to the end of our session, I'd just like to highlight the passages for the coming week, at the end of chapter six. You can always go back over the calming of the storm, if you like. Don't feel you have to get through all the passages — stay on any one passage for as long as it helps you..

And as usual, I want to encourage you all to make sure you get your special fifteen minutes each day. And I look forward to meeting you all again next _____ day and hearing how you get on. You're also asked to read chapter six during the coming week — again, it's quite short, but it will help a lot to have it read before the next session.

Before I pass around the 'secret bag,' can we have a volunteer to bring the snack next week?..

Pass the secret bag.

Well, that's the end of our session. Thank you very much for giving up your time to be here, and for the trust you've shown.

SESSION SIX

Checklist

Your handbook;

Your copy-book (with some notes on your week's prayer);

Bible, opened in a central position;

Cassette with suitable instrumental music, and cassette player;

This leader's guide;

Reading light (it can help the atmosphere during sharing and during prayer exercises to switch off the main light and use only a reading light);

Candle and matches;

'Secret bag' for donations;

Some blank sheets of paper (see section six).

1. Introduction

Welcome, everyone — and thanks for making the effort to come. Last week, we looked at how we can talk more from the heart, and this week we'll be looking at the effect of prayer, bearing in mind that actions speak louder than words.

I'd ask you, as usual, to make sure you're sitting beside people you weren't sitting next to before.

I'll light the candle now in front of the open Bible to remind us of the presence of Jesus, the light of the world, as we read the Word of God.

2. How we got on (20-30 minutes)

If the group is a quiet one, feel free to give them a few minutes first to chat in threes about how they got on during the week.

We'll move on now to take a little time on how you got on during the week. You can mention anything you like — there were various suggestions for getting down to prayer, like having your Bible marked and having a notebook and pen beside it, reading the next day's passage the evening before, noticing God noticing you, or listening to God tell you how you are loved. Then the main prayer — there have been various suggestions, like imagining the scene or listening to one of the characters, or finding a word or phrase and repeating it, or talking from the heart. You can mention how you're getting on with any of these things — or how you got on with the passages themselves, how you felt, or how any of the passages touched you personally — just a few of the more important points rather than a blow by blow account of the week.

Don't be afraid of silence — it may take a little while for people to get their thoughts together and to warm up. As usual, it can be helpful if the team also talk about their own prayer and about what is going on in their lives. That is especially useful if people are wandering off the subject and the sharing needs to be brought back on focus. Don't talk for long yourself — remember that your goal is to enable the others. Don't go beyond about 30 minutes on this section, or the rest of the session may suffer.

3. Introducing the new topic (5-10 minutes)

We'll move on now to the topic for this session, which is about the effects of prayer. We see that the real glory and honour we give to God is not mere words of praise but the quality of our lives and the way we live and love together. I hope you all got a chance to read chapter six — there's a summary of the tips from it at the end of the chapter, and you might like to take a minute or so to read them.

Ask everyone to open their books at the end of chapter four — at the summary of tips. Unless people have poor reading skills, you might allow a minute or so for them to read the tips for themselves. Allow time for reading.

After a minute or two:

I wonder if there was anything new for you in chapter six, or how you found it — or if you would like to comment on any of these tips?..

Encourage comments rather than questions, not by teaching, but by showing an openness to people's experience. So you might answer questions with: 'I wonder what does anyone else think about this, or what's your experience of it?' You might also feel free to make a few comments from your own experience on any of the tips. It's probably best not to delay on this section, but to move on quickly to the next section when they will have an actual experience of praying.

4. Quietening down (about 6-7 minutes)
As usual, we'll begin our prayer by relaxing and quietening down. I'll put on a little background music to help..

Play music, and dim lights.

Now, just as you did last week, become aware of your breathing, continuing to breathe as you have been, or, if you prefer, taking deeper, slower breaths. Keep your back fairly straight, but be peaceful, and relax, and notice your breathing. Any thoughts that come to you, just put them aside and keep concentrating on breathing in and out.

After about three minutes:

As you breathe in, you could say something like the name 'Jesus' or 'Come, Holy Spirit' or 'Come, Lord Jesus,' or 'Lord, teach us to pray' — whatever phrase appeals to you, and become aware of the presence of God within you, loving you and caring about you, and open yourself up to the Spirit teaching you to pray.. (one minute)

So, as you make that prayer, become aware of the presence of God within you... (one minute)

As you breathe out each time, you might hand over to God your life, your pressures, your guilt, your worries..

5. Praying with the New Testament (20-30 minutes)
We'll move on now to praying with the Scripture story for today. It usually helps us to meet Jesus when we take some time to imagine the scene, to look at Jesus, to listen to him, to ask ourselves how he feels at each stage.

Read slowly, pausing where there are continuous dots, to let people imagine:

You're standing beside a dirt track a little bit outside a country

village — can you see the village, with the synagogue rising a little
above the houses?.. Some of the houses look quite poor and shabby,
dirty white — can you see them?.. Now look at the sky. It's been
raining, and the sky is cloudy and overcast — can you see the clouds?..
Now look at the dirt track going into the hills — you can't see very far
because of the mist, but the track is muddy with big puddles right
across it in places... Become aware of a group of men waiting outside
the village — see them huddled together... Notice what leprosy has
done to a few of them — fingers missing, one man has lost his leg, part
of another's face is eaten away... Can you hear the tinkling of the bells
they wear to warn people to stay away in case they catch this dreaded
disease... Now see the hopelessness and misery in their eyes... Can you
sense the misery they feel , condemned to a terrible existence? One of
the men feels even more of an outcast because he's not liked by the
others — he's a Samaritan, and Jews and Samaritans hate each other.
Look at him — can you imagine how badly he feels?... The men have
heard that a travelling preacher is coming, and in their desperation
they'll try anything. They're pointing out along the track now —
there's a group of people heading in towards the village, coming closer
to you... As they come closer, you can see that their clothes are still
damp from the rain and spattered with mud... Jesus must be
somewhere at the back, for you can't see him. But look at the disciples'
faces. They look tired after their long walk. They'll be glad of a rest
and a bite to eat in the village... Now the disciples look frightened —
they've just seen the group of lepers near the road. They slow down...
Here's Jesus now, coming forward out of the crowd — what expression
do you see in his face?.. This is the moment the lepers had been
waiting for, hardly daring to hope. 'Jesus!' they call out, 'Master!'
'Jesus! Take pity on us!'... Jesus is calm, with great tenderness in his
face. Hear him telling them to go and show themselves to the priests...
Watch them turn away towards the village, puzzled, and probably
disappointed... As they walk, they are healed — look at the
astonishment and delight in their faces — what are they saying to each
other?.. The Samaritan turns around, tears in his eyes, and comes back

to Jesus... As he comes up, he can hardly speak with the emotion, but he is praising God who has cured him through this Jew, this enemy of his people — what words of praise can you hear him say?.. He comes right up to Jesus and looks at him, the tears now running down his cheeks. Words of thanks feel insufficient. He has been given a new life, an opportunity to start life again — how can he adequately express his thanks to this man with the kind steady eyes? He does something unexpected — he throws himself right down on the ground in front of Jesus and thanks him... See the sadness and disappointment in Jesus' eyes that so many others were given the opportunity to live a new life and just went their own way, unappreciative, unaware of Jesus, and of the extraordinary things God had done in their lives... Now see Jesus stooping down. The man feels Jesus touching him, raising him up off the ground, hugging him... Jesus speaks 'Your faith has made you well.' and at that moment the man feels a much deeper healing inside, and he knows that he really has begun a new life, a new journey of faith. He has been given a new heart...

After a longer pause:

Maybe you'd like to look at the passage in your book now, pick out a word or phrase that strikes you, and say it aloud..

As Jesus made his way to Jerusalem, he went along the border between Samaria and Galilee. He was going into a village when he was met by ten men suffering from a dreaded skin disease They stood at a distance and shouted, "Jesus! Master! Take pity on us!"

Jesus saw them and said to them, "Go and let the priests examine you."

On the way they were made clean. When one of them saw that he was healed, he came back praising God in a loud voice. He threw himself to the ground at Jesus' feet and thanked him. The man was a Samaritan. Jesus said, "There were ten men who were healed; where are the other nine? Why is this foreigner the only one who came back to give thanks to God?" And Jesus said to him, "Get up and go; your faith has made you well."

When everyone has spoken:

We'll take five or six minutes now to pray. You can pray on any of those phrases you've just heard, perhaps repeating them and letting them sink into your heart; or picture the scene, and let Jesus do and say to you what he does to the leper; or just be grateful for the ways that you have been healed and given a new life; or talk to Jesus about what the story is saying to you, remembering also to thank and praise him. Just pray whatever way the Spirit leads you...

After about three minutes, some may begin to lose concentration, so you might suggest:

If you like, as part of your prayer, you could repeat over and over again Jesus' words 'Your faith has made you well' — and experience the gift of faith and healing he is giving you...

After a few more minutes:

We've seen that it's not a good idea to spend our prayer time making plans, but now, as we come to the end of our prayer, it can be a good idea to take some time to make some little practical plan — some way of living this new life, this second chance, that has been offered to us, in our relationship with God and family and friends, particularly in the next few hours, or in the next day...

After about two minutes:

And we'll end our prayer now as usual by taking a minute more to thank God for all we have been given and to ask for the grace to carry out any plan we may have made.

Depending on what time is available, you might encourage anyone who wishes to make a prayer aloud:

Feel free now, anyone who wishes, to make a little prayer aloud — maybe a word of thanks or something that's on your mind, or something arising out of your prayer.

6. Summing up and comments (5-10 minutes)

Would you like to share now with two or three others how your prayer went — just share what you're comfortable with..

Allow about five minutes for this chat — depending on how relaxed and open they are with each other. Then:

We're coming now to the end of our last session, so I'd like to ask you, if you don't mind, to write on a sheet of paper one thing that you liked or learnt or gained from the course, and maybe one thing you weren't so happy about, or one change in the programme that might have made it better. You needn't put your name to what you write, so that you can be really honest in what you say, and we'll collect the sheets at the end. So feel free to say at least one positive thing, and one negative thing — you can be as brief as you like...

Allow a minute or two. Collect the sheets. Then:

And I would also like to invite you to say anything you like about your experience of the course — both negative and positive — either something you've written or something else you'd like to say...

7. Concluding remarks

Just before we finish, maybe you'd like to take a minute to have a little chat with the person beside you in order to plan ahead into the future — take a look at the suggestions in the 'Planning' section at the end of chapter six. You could ask yourselves what the main obstacles will be that you will meet, and how you could get around them, and you might write down what you decide...

(Allow about two minutes)

That brings us to the end of our course together, but obviously, regular prayer needs to continue. So I'd like to highlight the passages at the end of chapter six for the coming week. You're also asked to read the short chapter at the end of the book on where to go from here. That should give you some ideas on how to continue what has been begun here.

So I'll just pass around the 'secret bag' before I make my closing remarks.

Pass the secret bag. Both leaders might then say a few words of appreciation.

Well, I just want to finish by thanking you very much for giving up your time to be here, and for the trust you've shown. You

remember that the passage on the first evening was about Jesus coming into the upper room bringing the disciples his peace and joy, so I would like to give you all an opportunity to share that peace and joy with one another. You can feel free to use whatever sign of peace suits you — to hug or shake hands, or whatever...

Now, many people decide to work right through the course again in the privacy of their own homes, and they claim that they get a lot more out of it all that way. I don't know how many of you are interested in doing something like that, but, if you like, we could arrange to meet in six or seven weeks to talk about how you've been getting on...

If the participants want a further meeting, it can follow the same format — sharing of how things went since the previous meeting, then quietening down and practising prayer with a passage from the Bible, something like what they've been used to. But if they want to continue to meet on a regular basis, they may need to be encouraged to take responsibility for these meetings themselves.

SAMPLE LETTER INVITING PEOPLE TO ATTEND

Feel free to add to or adapt this letter. You may like to link it with a previous course on parenting, for example, or to add comments made by people who have already experienced the course.

Dear

Many people today seem to feel a need for some support for themselves or for their families in developing a deeper spiritual life. For example, they often feel dissatisfied with their own personal prayer and have a sense of not knowing how to pray. The truth is, of course, that the way they have always prayed is probably very good, but they may have come to a new stage when they need some simple, practical guidelines that might make their prayer more real, affect the way they live, and give more meaning to their lives.

Only God can teach us to pray. But it is helpful to have some outside support and the opportunity to practise different methods.

So I am writing to invite you to consider doing a simple, practical programme or 'retreat' on personal prayer. There will be six weekly sessions, lasting ninety minutes each, starting each _____ day at... You will be very welcome.

I think you will find this very practical and down to earth, for it has been used successfully with small groups of not more than ten people from all kinds of backgrounds. It is for ordinary people in any situation and from every walk of life.

There isn't just one way of praying — each person is different — so each one tends to find a way of praying that suits them personally. I think you will find, too, that your own privacy will be absolutely respected.

Because the group needs to be a small one, I need to know exact numbers in advance, so I would ask you to fill in the attached form if you would like to do the course. Those who are bringing along a friend are asked to put both names on the form. There is no charge, but there will be an opportunity to give a donation anonymously to cover any costs involved. The costs include a simple, attractive book that is provided for each participant — you will be asked to read a few pages of this book between sessions and to set aside 10-15 minutes each day for prayer while the programme or 'retreat' lasts.

Yours sincerely,

REPLY FORM — *please return to...*

*I/We wish to attend the "Enjoy praying" programme, starting on...
in...*

NAME(S): ....

ADDRESS: ....

Phone number...........................

61